Pablo Picasso
Master of Modern Art

Liz Gogerly

HODDER
Wayland

an imprint of Hodder Children's Books

© 2003 White-Thomson Publishing Ltd

Produced by White-Thomson Publishing Ltd
2/3 St Andrew's Place, Lewes, BN7 1UP

Editor: Elaine Fuoco-Lang
Inside and cover design: Tim Mayer
Picture Research: Shelley Noronha –
   Glass Onion Pictures
Proofreader: Jane Colgan

Cover: Pablo Picasso in 1973.
Title page: Pablo Picasso in his studio in 1935.

Published in Great Britain in 2003 by Hodder Wayland,
an imprint of Hodder Children's Books

Hodder Children's Books
An imprint of Hodder Headline Limited
338 Euston Road, London, NW1 3BH

Titles in this series:
Muhammad Ali: The Greatest
Neil Armstrong: The First Man on the Moon
Fidel Castro: Leader of Cuba's Revolution
Bill Gates: Computer Legend
Diana: The People's Princess
Martin Luther King Jr.: Civil Rights Hero
Nelson Mandela: Father of Freedom
Mother Teresa: Saint of the Slums
Pope John Paul II: Pope for the People
Queen Elizabeth II: Monarch of Our Times
The Queen Mother: Grandmother of a Nation
John Lennon: Voice of a Generation
Gandhi: The Peaceful Revolutionary
Florence Nightingale: The Lady of the Lamp
The Dalai Lama: Peacemaker from Tibet
Wolfgang Amadeus Mozart: Musical Genius
William Shakespeare: Poet and Playwright
Roald Dahl: The Storyteller
Elvis Presley: The King of Rock 'n' Roll
Vincent van Gogh: The Troubled Artist

British Library Cataloguing in Publication Data
Gogerly, Liz
   Picasso. - (Famous lives)
   1.Picasso, pablo, 1881-1973 - Juvenile literature
   2.Painters - spain - Biography - Juvenile literature
   I.Title
   759.6

ISBN 0 7502 4324 4

Printed in Hong Kong by Wing King Tong.

Picture acknowledgements:
AKG 14, 17, 19, 20, 33, 36; Bridgeman Art Library 6, 10,
12, 13, 15, 16, 21 Picasso, *The Family of Saltimbanques*,
1905, © Succession Picasso/DACS 2003, 23, 27, 32;
Camera Press 4, 7, 26, 41, 42, 45; Corbis 24; Hodder
Wayland Picture Library 28; Hulton Archive 11;
Popperfoto 30, 38, 39; Rex title page 31 Picasso, *Three
Musicians*, 1921, © Succession Picasso/DACS 2003, 34, 40;
Topham cover, 5, 8, 9, 18, 22, 25 Picasso, *Les Demoiselles
d'Avignon*, 1907, © Succession Picasso/DACS 2003, 29, 35,
37, 43, 44.

Contents

Guernica   4

A Spanish Childhood   6

Black-Eyed Boy   8

Taste of Freedom   10

The Magic of Paris   12

Bohemian Nights   14

Feeling Blue   16

Struggling to Survive   18

The Rose Period   20

Golden Days   22

Shock of the New   24

Invention of Cubism   26

The End of an Era   28

A Family Man   30

Surrealism by the Sea   32

Picasso's Women   34

An Ugly War   36

New Loves   38

Eye of a Genius   40

The Great Master   42

Picasso's Legacy   44

Glossary   46

Further Information   46

Date Chart   47

Index   48

Guernica

The Spanish Civil War had been raging since 1936. Then, in April 1937, German bombers destroyed the Spanish town of Guernica. When Pablo Picasso, the world-famous artist, heard the news, he was very angry. He began working on a painting he would call *Guernica*.

An old woman stands amongst the rubble of bombed buildings during the Spanish Civil War.

It wasn't until the centenary of Picasso's birth, on 25 October 1981, that **Guernica** was returned to Spain. It now hangs at the Reina Sofía, Spain's national museum of modern art.

> **'In the panel on which I am working and which I shall call Guernica, and in all my recent works of art, I clearly express my abhorrence [hatred] of the military caste [order] which has sunk Spain in an ocean of pain and death ...'** Picasso in May 1937.

On a huge canvas, Picasso painted humans and animals that were twisted and broken up into strange shapes. Their mouths were wide open as if they were screaming in agony. He used only black and white paint and shades of grey to paint the scene. When the painting was put on display at the Paris International Exhibition in July 1937, people were stunned. His powerful images said more than words ever could to show that war was a senseless waste of life.

A Spanish Childhood

Pablo Picasso was born at midnight on 25 October 1881 in Málaga, a seaside town in the south of Spain. At first, it seemed that he was born dead. But he survived, and this brush with death at the beginning of his life always fascinated Picasso.

A nineteenth-century engraving of Málaga from **The Picturesque Mediterranean.** *The round white building with the arches is the bullring.*

'When I was a child, my mother said to me, "If you become a soldier, you'll be a general. If you become a monk you'll end up as the pope." Instead I became a painter and wound up as Picasso.'
Picasso talking about the advice his mother gave him.

Picasso's father aged 32 years. He was a strong influence on Picasso and taught his son about art.

Picasso came from a poor but loving family. His father, José Ruiz Blasco, was a painter and art teacher who often struggled to support his family. His mother, Maria Picasso López, was warm-hearted and encouraged her son to become an artist. In 1884, Picasso's sister Lola was born. Another sister – Conchita – was born in 1887 but she died when she was seven years old.

From a young age Picasso's father took him to the bullring in Málaga. Picasso always enjoyed watching the battles between the bull and the toreador. The thrill of the bullfight never left Picasso. It was a drama of life and death, to which he would return in many of his paintings.

Black-Eyed Boy

Picasso's mother fondly recalled that Picasso could draw before he could speak properly. She also said that his first words were 'piz, piz' – a childish demand for a pencil. By the time Picasso was nine, his pencil drawings showed that his ability was far greater than other children of the same age.

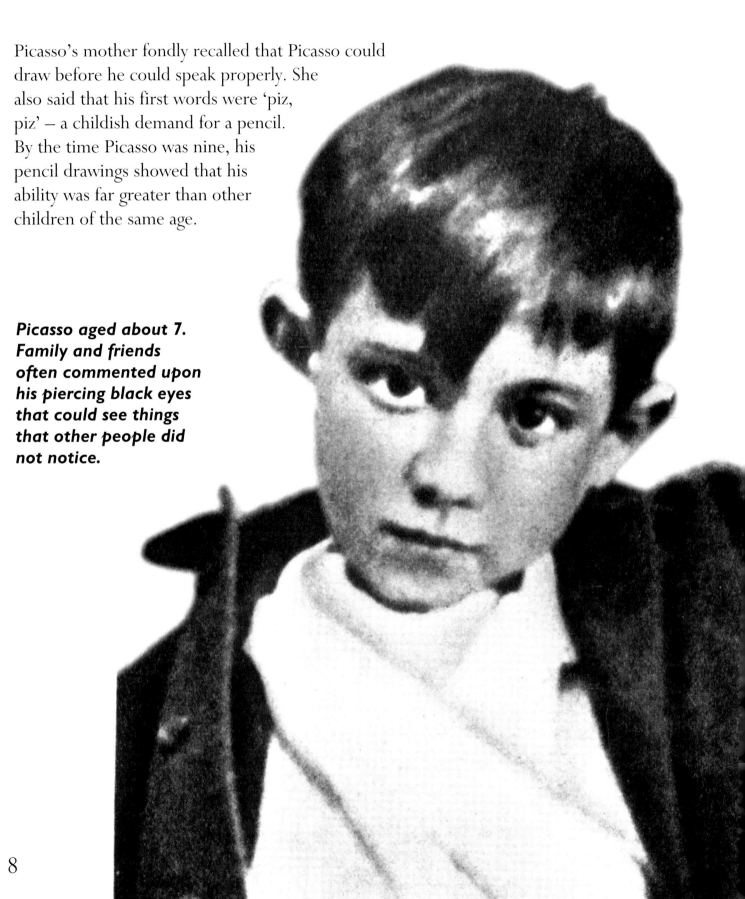

Picasso aged about 7. Family and friends often commented upon his piercing black eyes that could see things that other people did not notice.

Picasso's father was obsessed with drawing pigeons. Many of Picasso's paintings feature birds too. Here Picasso and his wife Jacqueline attend an exhibition of his work in Nice in 1961.

'For being a bad student, they would send me to the 'cells'... I loved it when they sent me there, because I could take a pad of paper and draw nonstop.' Picasso remembering his school days in La Coruña. From *Picasso: Creator and Destroyer.*

In 1891 the family moved to La Coruña on the north coast of Spain. Picasso's father took a job teaching at the Institute of Fine Arts. At school Picasso preferred doodling to paying attention in class. He was not very good at maths and, in later life, claimed he never learned the alphabet properly. His talent was for drawing and in 1892 he began formal art training at the Institute. But in 1895 the family moved to Barcelona. Picasso was only 14 but his entrance exam to the School of Fine Arts in Barcelona was so outstanding that he was accepted despite his young age.

9

Taste of Freedom

Throughout his full life, Picasso longed to do things his own way. When he studied at the School of Fine Arts in Barcelona he soon became fed up with its strict rules. When Picasso got bored, he would often escape the classroom to explore the streets of Barcelona. In October 1897, aged 16, he enrolled at the prestigious Royal Academy of San Fernando in Madrid.

A painting of nineteenth-century Madrid, where Picasso went to college in 1897.

However, it wasn't long before he was skipping classes so he could wander about Madrid's dark alleys sketching the scenes that interested him. Picasso preferred to draw what he saw in real life, such as gypsies and beggars, rather than the classical subjects that the Academy taught him.

In 1899 Picasso returned to Barcelona. His favourite place was a café called 'El Quatre Gats' (The Four Cats). Here Picasso could mingle with other artists, writers and poets. He sketched the customers and many of his pictures were pinned up on the walls of the café.

Barcelona at the beginning of the twentieth century. Picasso enjoyed living in Barcelona and socialising with new people who were interested in the arts.

The Magic of Paris

Picasso visited Paris for the first time in October 1900 with his friend, poet Carlos Casagemas. One of his paintings had been chosen for the Spanish Pavilion at the International Exhibition of 1900 which, for an unknown artist, was a great honour.

A postcard of the International Exhibition of 1900 in Paris. Many people came to see the Eiffel Tower lit up with electric lights.

The painting **Sunday Afternoon on the Island of La Grande Jatte** *is by Georges Pierre Seurat (1859–1891). He developed a technique known as Pointillism, whereby the whole painting was made up of tiny dots of colour.*

'It was in Paris I learned what a great painter Lautrec had been.'
Picasso talking about how Toulouse-Lautrec had inspired him. From *Picasso: Creator and Destroyer.*

In the 1860s, the great impressionist painters Claude Monet (1840-1926) and Auguste Renoir (1841-1919) had exhibited in Paris. They had shocked the art world with their new style of painting. For many years they were criticised and lived in poverty. By the 1880s their style had become more popular. Then post-impressionist painters such as Vincent van Gogh (1853-90), Paul Gauguin (1848-1903) and Henri de Toulouse-Lautrec (1864-1901) created new ways of painting with thick outlines and bright colours. Though many of these men were not famous until after they had died, they were an inspiration to young artists like Picasso.

Bohemian Nights

On 25 October 1899 Picasso celebrated his 19th birthday. He and Casagemas had been living in an area of Paris called Montmartre. It was a well-known place for penniless artists and writers to live. The cafés and bars were filled with chattering and laughing people. There was music and noise everywhere. Picasso had met up with a group of Spanish artists and most nights they went out together. With his boyish good looks and his charming personality, Picasso was always popular with women.

This postcard from 1898 shows the Moulin de la Galette. Picasso regularly visited the ballroom and did a painting of it on his first visit to Paris.

Picasso often copied the style of other painters. Picasso's painting of the Moulin de la Galette was influenced by Toulouse-Lautrec's painting, **The Dance at the Moulin Rouge** *pictured above.*

'Some nights we got to ... theatres ... Here everything is fanfare, full of tinsel and cloth made of cardboard and papier-mâché ...Whenever there is light ... we are in the studio painting and drawing.'
Casagemas writing about their life in Paris in a letter to a friend in Barcelona. From *Picasso: Creator and Destroyer.*

Life was fun and exciting but Picasso never forgot why he was in Paris. He continued to sketch and paint and experimented with the bright colours used by van Gogh and Lautrec. His work was noticed by an art dealer called Petrus Manyac who offered him 150 francs [approximately £15] a month for his paintings. Picasso accepted the deal but by Christmas 1899 he was ready to return to his family home in Málaga.

Feeling Blue

A painting of Madrid in 1900 by Enrique Martinez Cubells y Ruiz. Picasso was in Madrid when he heard about the death of his friend Casagemas.

It was wonderful to be back on the Mediterranean coast but Picasso found it difficult being around his family again. After just two weeks at home he left and went back to Madrid where he struggled to survive on the money from Manyac. Then in February he heard his friend Casagemas had shot himself in a café in Paris. Picasso was depressed and the only way he knew how to make himself feel better was to paint. But he still felt unsettled in Madrid and when he was asked to exhibit his work in Paris he decided to go back there.

'We all know that Art is not truth. Art is a lie that makes us realise truth.'
Picasso.

Poor areas of Montmartre, such as the one shown above, were where Picasso got much of his inspiration for his paintings during his Blue Period.

Picasso moved into a studio next to the café where Casagemas had killed himself. Once more Picasso was attracted to sketching the loneliness and misery that he saw on the streets of Montmartre. The paintings were sad and haunted because he only used shades of blues, greys and greens. This time is known as Picasso's Blue Period and it lasted until 1904.

Struggling to Survive

Picasso's friend, the poet Max Jacob, shown in later life.

Today Picasso's paintings from the Blue Period hang in famous art galleries around the world. *Child Holding a Dove*, *The Tragedy* and *Woman in a Chemise* can be seen by millions of people. When he painted these pictures no one would buy them. His depression deepened as he moved from one cheap room to another. Many of his artist friends were poor too but Picasso often relied upon their generosity. In 1902 the poet Max Jacob allowed him to move into his tiny studio room for a few months. They shared a bed, each small meal and even their clothes.

Poverty and lack of success made Picasso restless. He moved between Paris and Barcelona searching for success. In April 1904 he finally decided to make Paris his permanent home. He rented a room in an old piano factory that a friend had called the Bateau Lavoir (Laundry Boat). The run-down building was filled with artists, writers, students and workers. It was overcrowded and noisy, and Picasso's room was filthy. Yet, out of this squalor, came happiness and success.

The entrance to the Bateau Lavoir in Montmartre, as it looked in 1939. Picasso often said his years there were the happiest time of his life.

The Rose Period

Picasso's cluttered room was filled with junk, furniture and canvases. Before long he had three dogs, a cat and a white mouse. He made new friends, like the poets Guillaume Apollinaire and André Salmon. His days were spent socialising in cafés and bars. Then at night he worked frantically, producing hundreds of paintings. At this time Picasso met the beautiful Fernande Oliver on the stairs of the Bateau Lavoir. They fell in love and she moved into his studio. For the first time in years he felt happy.

087. — PARIS - Vieux-Montmartre - Cabaret artistique du Lapin Agile   J. H.

Picasso was a regular customer at the café, Le Lapin Agile. He painted a picture of himself at the bar in 1905 called Au Lapin Agile.

20

Picasso

A *study* for the *painting* The Family of Saltimbanques, *showing a group of circus performers.*

Picasso's new-found happiness began to affect his work. The dark blues and greens in his paintings were replaced with reds and pinks. His paintings from 1905 to 1906 are now recognized as his Rose Period. One of the most famous paintings from this time is *The Family of Saltimbanques*.

Golden Days

Picasso's paintings were hung next to those of his rival Henri Matisse once again in 2002 and 2003, in a major exhibition that toured the world. A Picasso self-portrait from 1906 (left) hangs next to a self-portrait by Matisse.

Picasso lived at the Bateau Lavoir for five years. While most artists were eager to exhibit their work, Picasso refused to show his paintings to the public. He could have made money by illustrating magazines but Picasso believed his talents were too great for this type of work.

'The first picture we had of his ... **The Young Girl with a Basket of Flowers**, it was painted ... full of grace and delicacy and charm. After that little by little his drawing hardened, his line become firmer, his color more vigorous ...' Gertrude Stein describing Picasso's changing style after the Rose Period. From *Picasso: Creator and Destroyer.*

In 1904 Picasso's luck began to change. The art dealer Ambroise Vollard bought thirty of his paintings. Then in 1905 he met the American brother and sister Leo and Gertrude Stein. They lived in Paris and collected paintings by new artists. They began buying Picasso's paintings and hung them on the walls of their apartment next to the work of other artists, such as Paul Cézanne (1839-1906) and Henri Matisse (1869-1954). Suddenly, at the age of 25, Picasso's work was in demand and his days as a poor artist were over. Yet he still wasn't satisfied and he searched for a new way of expressing himself.

The Post-Impressionist painter Paul Cézanne painted this picture **Rocks** *in 1904. His modern style influenced Picasso.*

Shock of the New

In the spring of 1906, Picasso persuaded Gertrude to pose for a portrait. He was able to paint her body but he couldn't get her face quite right. Overwhelmed by frustration, he left for a holiday in Spain and painted her face from memory when he got back. Her face wasn't a true likeness: it was more like a primitive mask. His friends were critical of the unflattering painting but Gertrude liked it.

'... everybody thinks she is not at all like her portrait but never mind, in the end she will manage to look just like it.'
Picasso's reaction to criticism of his portrait of Gertrude Stein. From *Picasso: Creator and Destroyer*.

Gertrude Stein sits beneath her portrait by Picasso. Many people thought Gertrude looked more like her portrait as she got older.

Picasso painted Les Demoiselles d'Avignon in 1907 but it wasn't shown to the public until 1916. It was not until the 1930s that its importance was appreciated.

Picasso was inspired. In spring 1907 Picasso gathered his close friends at his studio to show them his new painting: *Les Demoiselles d'Avignon*. When he revealed his painting, they were shocked to see five naked women with back-to-front bodies and mask-like faces. This revolutionary painting is now recognized as the beginning of modern art.

Invention of Cubism

Picasso continued to paint in the same style as he had with *Les Demoiselles d'Avignon*. He worked closely with the French artist Georges Braque (1882-1963) and together they created a new painting style that would be called Cubism. Everyday objects became a collection of cubes and geometric shapes. When Picasso painted the art dealer Daniel-Henry Kahnweiler, it was almost impossible to recognize him. Cubism was criticised but it also captured the imaginations of artists all around the world.

Picasso's friend Georges Braque in 1909 at Picasso's studio. Picasso described them as being like two rock climbers tied together. He meant that their work was so closely linked that if one of them made a mistake it would have a direct effect on the other.

Collectors from all round the world were buying Picasso's work and he had enough money to live well. However, he waited until 1909 before he moved to a luxury apartment in a better part of Paris. There he employed a maid but wouldn't allow her to dust in case it settled on his precious canvases.

'Painting is freedom. If you jump, you might fall on the wrong side of the rope. But if you're not willing to take the risk of breaking your neck, what good is it? You don't jump at all. You have to wake people up.'
Picasso describing his work. From *Picasso: Creator and Destroyer.*

Picasso in his studio with a sketch for one of his Cubist paintings behind him.

The End of an Era

Fernande was jealous of the time Picasso spent with Braque and they split up in 1912. Picasso then fell in love with Marcelle Humbert. Picasso and Marcelle spent happy holidays in Spain and the south of France and life was good. Braque and Picasso continued to experiment with Cubism. They glued anything from newspaper, wallpaper, pieces of rope and cardboard to their pictures in a style that became known as Collage. But in 1914 the First World War began and life changed for everybody.

Parisiennes gather in the street to watch German planes fly over France during the First World War (1914-18).

Many of Picasso's friends went off to fight. Picasso couldn't join them because he was Spanish and the war did not involve Spain. Then in 1916 Marcelle died. It was a bleak lonely time for Picasso. But his spirits were raised when he visited Rome in Italy in 1917 to work on the costumes and scenery for the ballet *Parade*. He worked alongside the great ballet impresario Sergei Diaghilev, his close friend and playwright Jean Cocteau and composer Erik Satie.

'He is small in stature and built like a bull-fighter. His skin is sallow and his wicked black eyes are set close together; the mouth is strong and finely drawn. He reminded me of a racehorse ...'
A Danish art critic describes Picasso's appearance in 1916.
From *A Life of Picasso 1907-1917: The Painter of Modern Life*.

Picasso (left) with Jean Cocteau at a bullfight in Barcelona in 1956. They were close friends until Cocteau's death in 1963.

A Family Man

Picasso and Olga in 1919. For a short while, under Olga's influence, he ordered suits from the best tailors.

In Rome Picasso met the woman that helped him forget Marcelle. Olga Koklova was a ballet dancer in Diaghilev's Russian ballet. They travelled to Madrid and Barcelona together. When they were married in July 1918, many of Picasso's friends thought their marriage was doomed from the start.

In **Three Musicians** *of 1921, Picasso formed figures from blocks of bright colours. Behind the figure on the left is the shape of a dog, which merges with the floor and table.*

'Braque is the wife who loved me most.'
Picasso often joked that he was closer to his fellow artist and friend Georges Braque than he was to any of his wives. *From Picasso: His Life and Work.*

In November 1918 the First World War ended. The newly-weds moved into an elegant villa in Paris. Picasso's happiness was reflected in his paintings such as *Three Musicians* and *Still Life on a Table*. When Picasso's first son Paolo was born in 1921, Picasso seemed to have settled down to enjoy family life. Though he was rich, he still preferred to wear ragged clothes and his studio was always messy and full of canvases and his collection of interesting bits and pieces.

Surrealism by the Sea

During the 1920s, the influence of Cubism spread to architecture, fashion and furniture. There were new movements in art too. Surrealism allowed artists to move away from traditional styles. The Spanish Surrealist artist, Salvador Dali (1904-89), painted dream-like pictures, such as deserts filled with dead trees and melting clocks. Picasso never claimed to belong to any art group but he was inspired by everything, and continued to produce a huge amount of work.

Picasso stands in front of his canvases in about 1929. Sketches from the Bathers series can be seen scattered on the floor.

These people are enjoying the French seaside in 1929. Picasso loved to watch people enjoying themselves on the beach.

'Painting is a blind man's profession. He paints not what he sees, but what he feels, what he tells himself about what he has seen.'
Picasso talking about his art. From *The New Penguin Dictionary of Modern Quotations*.

Picasso was now middle-aged and could afford to spend his summers in luxury by the coast. He enjoyed the calm of the seaside and was inspired by the sea and watching other people relaxing on the beach. In a series of paintings called *Bathers* he showed how Surrealism had influenced his work. In 1931 he bought a seventeenth-century château at Boisgeloup, close to Paris. He set up his studio in the stables there and began creating metal sculptures made from everyday objects he found around him.

Picasso's Women

As his friends had predicted the marriage between Picasso and Olga did not last. In 1927 he met another woman called Marie-Thérèse Walter by chance in the street. When she became pregnant in 1935, Olga left Picasso, taking Paolo with her. Maya, Picasso's daughter with Marie-Thérèse, was born in 1935 but the following year Picasso met an intelligent and beautiful photographer called Dora Maar and conducted an affair with her at the same time.

Picasso sitting alone in his studio in about 1935. Though Picasso loved the company of women, he was often moody and cruel to them.

One of Picasso's paintings of Marie-Thérèse Walter arrives at Christie's auction house in London in 2002 and sells for nearly £15 million.

Women always played a major part in Picasso's life. When he fell in love, it was with passion. The women he loved became the models for his paintings, and he would paint beautiful pictures of them. When he fell out of love with them, his paintings showed them to be ugly and disgusting. Picasso painted Olga in a classical style, but when Picasso painted Marie-Thérèse he chose to use a more Cubist style (like the painting shown above). The soft lines of this picture shows how much he was in love with his subject at that time.

An Ugly War

Picasso was living in Paris when the Nazis occupied the French capital in June 1940. Picasso was invited to emigrate to America but he decided to stay. Living in wartime Paris was tough; fuel was rationed and art materials were in short supply, but Picasso still painted as much as he could. Many of his paintings were dark and gloomy, and revealed his hatred of the war. *Still Life with Ox Skull* is one of a series of paintings where he paints animal skulls. Picasso was also sad to have lost so many of his friends in the war, including the poet Max Jacob who had died in a Nazi concentration camp.

Adolf Hitler (centre) visits occupied Paris on 28 June, 1940.

Picasso poses with his arm around one of his life-size sculptures in his Paris studio in 1944.

Picasso hated the Nazis and had friends in the French Resistance. He loved telling the story of how a Nazi officer had entered his studio and asked him about a photograph of his anti-war painting *Guernica* (in which he depicted the Nazi destruction of the Spanish town, see pages 4-5). When the officer asked him if he'd done the picture, Picasso had replied, 'No … you did'. Many people thought he was very brave to remain in Paris. When the war ended in 1945, Picasso was surprised how his reputation had grown.

New Loves

Following the war, Picasso lived mainly in the south of France near the sea. His love life became more complicated. He received nasty letters from Olga, he frequently argued with Dora, and Marie-Thérèse longed for him to love her again. Picasso spent most of his time working in a new style of art called lithography. This process meant that an original engraving could be reproduced hundreds of times, which made his work more affordable. While he was working on lithographs, Picasso met and fell in love with a 21-year-old artist called Françoise Gilot.

Picasso holds up one of the plates he has decorated at an exhibition of his work in Paris in 1948.

'One starts to get young at the age of sixty and then it is too late.'
Picasso in an interview with *The Sunday Times* from *The New Penguin Dictionary of Modern Quotations*.

Picasso was fond of children and enjoyed teaching his children, Claude and Paloma, to draw. This picture taken in 1953 shows how they practised drawing pigeons, just like Picasso had done as a child.

Now in his sixties, Picasso became a father again. In 1947 Françoise gave birth to a baby boy called Claude and in 1949 she had a girl called Paloma. During these years Picasso experimented with ceramics, often inventing new ways of working in clay. He also began giving his works to museums. In the past, because of the shocking nature of some of his material, museums hadn't bought his works. Now curators were asking Picasso to donate his paintings because they couldn't afford to buy them.

Eye of a Genius

Françoise Gilot and her children had been a source of great happiness and inspiration for Picasso's bright and colourful paintings. But, after the birth of Paloma, he seemed to lose interest in his family and in 1953 Françoise left Picasso. He moved to a large villa in the hills above Cannes in the south of France. Picasso had become the first celebrity artist and fans often gathered in front of his home to try and meet him. He preferred a quiet life and only special friends, or other famous people, were invited through the gates into his home.

As he grew older, Picasso rarely left his home other than to visit bullfights in Spain.

Picasso with his second wife, Jacqueline, in his studio at his country house, Notre Dame de Vie, at Mougins just outside Cannes. Behind Picasso is a painting from 1931 called **Figures by the Sea.**

> **'Today, as you know, I am famous and very rich. But when I am alone with myself, I haven't the courage to consider myself an artist, in the great and ancient sense of that word ... I am only a public entertainer, who understands his age.'**
> Picasso interviewed in *Le Spectacle du monde* in 1962.

Picasso met Jacqueline Roque in 1954 and she became his model for most of his later works. They were married in 1961, and moved to a villa outside Cannes where he could concentrate on his work. By now he was experimenting with all kinds of mediums. His sculptures were often made from old bits of metal or rubbish. His ability to see life in everyday objects and turn them into new works of art was amazing.

The Great Master

While Picasso's paintings attracted much attention, he preferred to remain in his studio. Even though he was 84 when this photograph was taken, he was still working hard.

During the 1960s, Picasso's work was exhibited throughout the world. One of the most memorable exhibitions was in 1966 when over 700 of his works were shown in different galleries in Paris. By this time Picasso had become a recluse and did not visit the exhibition. On the opening day he amused himself thinking about other painters going to see his works. He'd grown tired of life and he asked, 'Painting, exhibiting – what's it all about?'

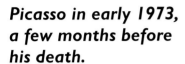

Picasso in early 1973, a few months before his death.

'Picasso is what is going to happen and what is happening.'
In 1970 the Mexican poet Octavio Paz described the energetic influence that Picasso had on the world of art, showing how his popularity has continued over the years.

In his final years Picasso's eyesight and hearing started to fail. Though he refused to see many of his relatives, including his children, he never lost his creative energy. Later paintings, such as *The Kiss* or *The Couple,* were as original and powerful as his early works. In 1972 he painted his last self-portrait. It was of an old man with a face contorted with pain. Picasso died at his home in Notre Dame de Vie in Mougins, France on 8 April 1973 at the age of 91.

Picasso's Legacy

Picasso was buried in the grounds of one of his homes, the Château of Vauvenargues in Provence, France. He left behind much sadness and tragedy. On the day of his funeral his grandson, also named Pablo, drank bleach and died three months later. In 1977 a frail and depressed Marie-Thérèse hanged herself aged 68. In 1986 Jacqueline, his last wife who had inherited his fortune, shot herself.

The final resting place of Pablo Picasso is in the secluded grounds of his home in Provence, the Château de Vauvenargues. On the day of his burial it snowed.

'God is really the only other artist. He invented the giraffe, the elephant, and the cat. He has no real style. He just keeps on trying other things.' Pablo Picasso in *Life with Picasso*.

The public's fascination with Picasso goes on and on. Exhibitions of his work still draw enormous crowds.

Picasso was a man of many contradictions. He was a Spaniard who adopted France as his homeland. He was charming and witty yet cruel and often depressed. He founded a new movement in art called Cubism but disliked being labelled as any kind of artist. He became a multi-millionaire but preferred to wear his bohemian rags. Art critics are divided about his work – was he a genius or merely in the right place at the right time? Most agree that his best works are *Guernica* and *Les Demoiselles d'Avignon*. Whatever we think of Pablo Picasso and his work, he has become one of the most idolized artists who ever lived.

Glossary

avant-garde New and innovative art or literature – often ahead of its time.

bohemian An untraditional social style.

canvas A strong coarse kind of cloth that is often used as a surface for oil-painting.

catalyst Something that causes change.

ceramics The art of making clay products.

civil war A war between different groups of people living in the same country.

classical Traditional way of doing things.

curator A person who looks after and selects objects for exhibitions/museums.

emigrate To move from the country where you were born to live in another country.

engraving A design that is cut into metal, wood or glass.

francs Old money used in France.

French Resistance The underground movement formed in France during the Second World War.

impresario an organizer of events.

Impressionist An artistic style that focused on colour and light to give an impression of a scene.

lithography Making prints from a stone or metal surface.

period Certain time in history.

prestigious Powerful, successful with an excellent reputation.

primitive Uncivilized, basic and simple.

prodigy A person with extraordinary talents or abilities.

recluse A person who prefers to live alone and rarely sees other people.

squalor Poor and filthy surroundings.

Surrealism A twentieth-century avant-garde movement in art and literature. Surrealist artists used images from dreams in their works.

toreador A bullfighter.

Further Information

Books for Children:

Life Times: Pablo Picasso by Liz Gogerly (Belitha, 2002)

Picasso by Peter Harrison (Hodder Wayland, 2001)

Picasso by Juliet Haslewood (Belitha, 2002)

Artists in Their Time: Picasso by Kate Scarborough (Franklin Watts, 2002)

Sources:

The New Penguin Dictionary of Modern Quotations by Robert Andrews (Penguin, 2001)

Picasso: His Life and Work by Roland Penrose (University of California Press, 1981)

A Life of Picasso 1907-1917: The Painter of Modern Life by John Richardson (Jonathan Cape, 1996)

Picasso: Creator and Destroyer by Arianna S. Huffington (Weidenfeld and Nicolson, 1988)

Date Chart

1881, 25 October Pablo Ruiz Blasco Picasso is born in Málaga, Spain.

1891 Picasso's family moves to La Coruña on the Atlantic coast of Spain. Picasso begins to study under his father.

1895 Picasso's family moves to Barcelona. Picasso attends the School of Fine Arts.

1897 Picasso attends the Royal Academy of San Fernando in Madrid.

1900, October Picasso visits Paris for the first time with his friend Carlos Casagemas.

1901-04 Picasso's Blue Period.

1905-06 Picasso's Rose Period. He falls in love with Fernande Oliver.

1907 Picasso paints *Les Demoiselles d'Avignon* – the painting now considered to be the beginning of modern art. He works with Georges Braque and experiments with a style of painting that is later called Cubism.

1908 Picasso and Braque's Cubist paintings are exhibited in Paris.

1912 Picasso and Braque experiment with Collage, Picasso splits up with Fernande and falls in love with Marcelle Humbert.

1914 The First World War begins.

1917 Picasso works with Jean Cocteau, Erik Satie and Sergei Diaghilev on a production of the ballet *Parade*. He travels to Rome and meets Olga Koklova.

1918, July Picasso marries Olga Koklova.
November The First World War ends.

1921 Picasso's first son, Paolo, is born.

1935 Marie-Thérèse gives birth to Picasso's first daughter Maya, Picasso splits with his wife Olga.

1936 The Spanish Civil War begins.

1937, April The bombing of the town of Guernica in Spain inspires Picasso to paint his great anti-war painting *Guernica.*

1939, September The Second World War begins; death is the subject of many of Picasso's paintings. He meets Françoise Gilot and works on lithographs.

1940 The Nazis occupy Paris.

1947 Françoise Gilot gives birth to Picasso's second son, Claude. Picasso moves to the south of France.

1949 Françoise Gilot gives birth to Picasso's second daughter, Paloma.

1953 Picasso and Françoise split up.

1954 Picasso meets Jacqueline Roque.

1961 Picasso marries Jacqueline Roque.

1966 Over 700 of Picasso's works are displayed in Paris in honour of his 85th birthday.

1971 Picasso becomes the first living artist to have his works on display at the Louvre in Paris.

1973, 8 April Picasso dies in his villa Notre Dame de Vie, Mougins, aged 91.

1980 A major exhibition of his work is held at the Museum of Modern Art in New York City.

2002 A major exhibition of the works of Picasso and his rival Matisse begins its tour of the world.

Index

All text in **bold** refers to pictures as well as text.

Bateau Lavoir **19**, 20, 22
Bathers **32**, 33
Blasco, José Ruiz (father) **7**, 9
Blue Period 17, 18
Braque, Georges 26, 28, 31
bullfighting 7, **29**, **40**

Casagemas, Carlos 12, 14, 15, 16, 17
Cezanne, Paul **23**
Child Holding a Dove 18
Cocteau, Jean **29**
Cubism 26-27, 28, 32, **35, 45**

Dali, Salvador 32
Dance at the Moulin Rouge, The 15
Demoiselles d'Avignon, Les **25**, 45
Diaghilev, Sergei 29, 30

Family of Saltimbanques **21**
First World War 28-29, 31

Gauguin, Paul 13
Gilot, Françoise 38, **39**, 40
Guernica 4, **5**, 37, 45

Humbert, Marcelle 28, 29

impressionism 13

Jacob, Max **18**, 36

Kiss, The 43
Koklova, Olga see Picasso, Olga

Maar, Dora 34, 35, 38
Matisse, Henri **22**, 23
Monet, Claude 13
Montmartre 14, **17**

Oliver, Fernande 20, 28

Parade, the ballet 29
Picasso, Claude (son) 39
Picasso, Jacqueline (wife) 9, 41, 44
Picasso López, Maria (mother) 6, 7, 8
Picasso, Olga (wife) **30**, 34, 38
Picasso, Pablo 6, **8**, **9**, 22, **27**, **30**, **32**, 33, **38**, **39**, **42**, **43**
   art training 9, 10-11
   childhood 7, 8-9
   children 31, 34, **39**, 40, 43
   women and 14, 20, 28, **30**, 34-35, 38

Picasso, Maya (daughter) 34
Picasso, Pablo (grandson) 44
Picasso, Paloma (daughter) **39**, 40
Picasso, Paolo (son) 31, 34
post-impressionism 13

Renoir, Auguste 13
Rose Period 20-21

Satie, Erik 29
School of Fine Arts, Barcelona 9, 10
sculpture 33, **37**, 41
Second World War 36-37
Seurat, Georges **13**
Spanish Civil War 4
Stein, Gertrude 22, 23, **24**
Still Life on a Table 31
Still Life with Ox Skull 36
Surrealism 32, 33

Three Musicians **31**
Toulouse-Lautrec, Henri de 13
Tragedy, The 18

van Gogh, Vincent 13, 15

Walter, Marie-Thérèse 34, **35**, 38, 44
Woman in a Chemise 18